An enamel sign used to promote the call-office service of the National Telephone Company. The detail was in blue on a white ground.

TELEPHONE BOXES

Neil Johannessen

Shire Publications Ltd

CONTENTS

Published in 1994 by Shire Publications Ltd, Cromwell House, Church Street, Princes Risborough, Buckinghamshire HP27 9AA, UK. Copyright © 1994 by Neil Johannessen. First edition 1994. Shire Album 303. ISBN 0 7478 0250 5.

All rights reserved. No part of this publication may be reproduced or transmitted in any form or by any means, electronic or mechanical, including photocopy, recording, or any information storage and retrieval system, without permission in writing from the publishers.

British Library Cataloguing in Publication Data: Johannessen, Neil. Telephone Boxes. – (Shire Albums; No. 303). I. Title II. Series. 717. ISBN 0-7478-0250-5.

Printed in Great Britain by CIT Printing Services, Press Buildings, Merlins Bridge, Haverfordwest, Dyfed SA61 1XF.

ACKNOWLEDGEMENTS

I am indebted to many individuals and organisations for their help in the production of this book, including BT, Mercury Communications, Neville Conder, Steve Walker, Dave Shapland, Dave Evans, Graham Wootten and Bolton Reference Library. To these and the many others who have contributed, I offer my sincere gratitude. Three individuals deserve particular mention: Andrew Hurley, who made the Avoncroft Museum kiosk display possible – without the excitement of that project, the book would not have been written; Stuart Churcher, who did most of the research on which it is based and without whose work it could never have been written; and, lastly, my young daughter. This book is for Hazel.

Cover: *Reproduced from a 1930s GPO poster used to help promote acceptance of the new red telephone kiosk. Many rural communities then thought it an inappropriate intrusion in the environment. How times change.*

This ornate iron box was operated by an attendant employed by the National Telephone Company. The site is today one of the entrances to Chancery Lane underground station, London.

THE EARLY YEARS

Britain's first telephone exchanges opened at the end of the 1870s, providing a service for members only. To use the telephone one had to be a subscriber. The idea of using the new system on a pay-by-the-call basis came later when, in 1884, non-subscribers were first allowed to use the telephone.

The 'call office' had arrived. To begin with, call offices were indoors, often in shops, where proprietors offered the facility as a service to their customers and an attraction to new ones. As the telephone system grew, sites at other public places, such as railway stations and post offices, also began to be used. Subscribers, whose annual fee included unlimited calls, were provided with identity tokens to enable them to use the offices without charge. Call offices first appeared as street telephone boxes around the beginning of the twentieth century. Some continued the practice of providing an attended service, but others relied on coin-in-the-slot devices on the door to collect the call fee.

There was no single design of box.

There were far too few for any economy of scale in their manufacture. Nevertheless, the telephone system was growing. The requirements of a good telephone box were beginning to be better understood and so, even though the numbers concerned were tiny in comparison with today, three main styles of kiosk became predominant: the 'Wilson', named after its manufacturer, and the 'Birmingham' and 'Norwich' patterns, named after the areas where they originated. All three were made of wood.

The National Telephone Company (NTC) provided by far the majority of Britain's telephones and exchanges, but only under a 31-year licence granted by the government in 1880. Its trunk system had been taken into state control in 1896, and in 1905 the company was told that its licence would not be renewed when it expired. Except in Hull and Portsmouth, where telephones were provided by the local council, from the end of 1911 the Post Office (GPO) would be responsible for the entire telephone network. The two

3

Bolton, 1905. One of the earliest confirmed street telephone boxes, this NTC box was one of two in Victoria Square, opposite the town hall. The second one was operated in competition by the Post Office.

local authority systems would remain in local hands, linking into the Post Office network for long-distance calls. The Portsmouth system remained independent for only a very little while longer, being sold to the Post Office in 1913. Hull continued as the only locally managed system.

With uniform control came moves towards uniform practice. The GPO and NTC staff were merged, stores and accounting systems were standardised, and thought turned to production of a standard design of telephone kiosk. The GPO looked at the models that were already in use and preferred the Birmingham pattern. Work began to see how a more ornamental version of it might be developed. Perhaps it might be painted red and be made of materials other than wood. However, it was not until after the First World War that the plans finally came to fruition.

The Wilson Company of Southsea manufactured one of the more numerous early telephone boxes. The 'Wilson A' pattern was its most popular model.

Below left: *The 'Norwich' pattern kiosk. It is believed that this photograph was taken during the GPO's review of the available designs.*
Below right: *This 'Birmingham' unit was finished with varnish. There was no standard colour or finish at the time.*

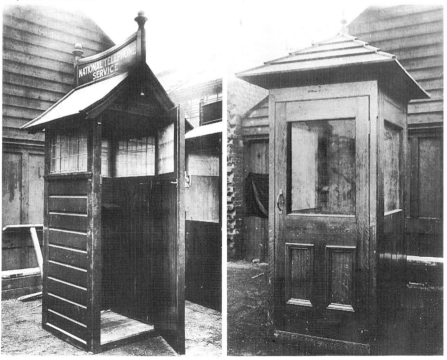

'K' FOR KIOSK

The concrete Kiosk No. 1, as introduced in 1921. It was made up in sections of reinforced concrete and fitted with a wooden door. The upper portion had glazed panels on the two sides and front. The three concrete sections fit into the base and top, all joints being filled in with cement. The first model, the Mk234, had wooden window frames. These were soon replaced by metal frames, in the Mk235.

The first standard kiosk – the Kiosk No. 1, or K1 – was a simple design. Little more than a modified Birmingham pattern, albeit made of pre-cast concrete, it did little to encourage the many local authorities to allow it on to their streets. The Post Office chose the proposed sites with great care, with situations off the main pavement being preferred. Frequently they resorted to striking a deal with a private landowner. They would even paint the box in whatever colour the local authority wanted. Even so, some were not to be persuaded and notable amongst these were the Metropolitan Boroughs, which controlled the central districts of London.

One concern was that telephone boxes were an obstruction to the thoroughfare and yet, somewhat oddly, what appeared to be called for was something grand and imposing. In 1923 the Metropolitan Boroughs Joint Standing Committee organised a design competition. The entries were disappointing and, in any case, more general discussion had begun. The Birmingham Civic Society had submitted a design to the Post Office, which had itself been busy, both with improvements to the K1 and in developing alternative design ideas.

Then the newly formed Royal Fine Arts Commission became involved. It had been established to advise on matters of public amenity and the Postmaster General invited the Commission to organise a further competition. A limited contest was arranged.

The Post Office and the Birmingham designs were carried forward, and three eminent architects were asked to submit further designs. The design brief recommended that the boxes should be constructed in cast iron and set a maximum unit cost of £40. Full-size models in wood of the five designs were lined up for judging on land behind the National Gallery. The general design of Giles Gilbert Scott was favoured and, with some modifications to ease manufacture, the new kiosk was introduced in 1926. It was designated the Kiosk No. 2. It was painted 'vermilion red' outside and 'flame' inside, and weighed over a ton. It was very imposing.

Scott's classically inspired design was neat and effective. A pierced crown appeared on all four sides to provide both ventilation and a visual link with the royal crest that decorated the GPO's letter boxes. The kiosk had no unnecessary decoration and featured an elegant dome that was to become an essential element in British kiosk design for half a century. It is said that Scott was inspired by the saucer dome above the tomb of Sir John Soane in St Pancras churchyard, or perhaps by the similar lantern at the Dulwich Picture Gallery. More probably his dome qualifies as a design classic, the perfect top to a small square building that is very much taller than it is wide.

The Post Office intended to use the K2 almost exclusively in London and, as boxes in the first production batch cost over £50 each, it determined that other places would get them only in the most special circumstances. This policy was largely successful: of more than 1500 K2s, only a few dozen or so were installed on sites outside London.

The K2 was not only too expensive for general use, it was also too big. With these factors in mind, the Post Office decided to continue to supply the K1, but in a dramatically remodelled form. Designated the K1 Mk236 and introduced in 1927, it had glazing reminiscent of Giles Gilbert Scott's design and was painted cream, with red glazing bars and a red door.

Over 5000 modified K1s were erected over the next three years while, in search of a better design, the Post Office asked Scott (by now Sir Giles) to design a further kiosk. The idea was to combine the smaller size and lower cost of the K1 with the quality of design of his K2. The result was the concrete K3. Introduced in 1929, it was similar in style to the K2. The K3 was to be the standard kiosk for Britain, a role it fulfilled very well. Around 12,000 units were erected all over the country during the next six years.

The K4, introduced in 1927, was a departure from the main run of kiosk development. It was a rather grand idea on the part of the Post Office, aiming to combine some of the services of a post office with a telephone kiosk, in a form of 24-hour post office. To achieve this they literally 'stretched' the K2, the additional space being used to accommodate a letter box and two stamp-vending machines. The K4 was rapidly nicknamed the 'Vermilion Giant'.

The K5, introduced in 1934, was even

Two of the 1923 competition entries. There were some innovative ideas but they were generally little more than reworkings of the 'Birmingham' and K1 designs.

The telephone boxes in the 1924 contest by (top left) the Birmingham Civic Society, (top right) Giles Gilbert Scott, (bottom left) Sir Robert Lorimer, (bottom centre) the GPO, and (bottom right) Sir John Burnet. After judging, four of the five wooden mock-ups went into public service, in covered sites. The Birmingham model appears to have been returned. Of the four that were put to use, one has miraculously survived. Under the courtyard arch entrance at the Royal Academy, Piccadilly, London, Scott's design can still be used.

Left: *New roof and door signs, introduced in 1924, did little to improve the basic K1.*

Right: *An early issue Kiosk No. 2. Giles Gilbert Scott envisaged that his design would be fabricated in steel, painted silver and have elegant serif lettering. The GPO chose to make it in cast iron, to paint it vermilion red, and to use their then normal blue and white kiosk lettering.*

more of a departure. In some ways it was not even a real kiosk. Made in steel-faced plywood, it was a transportable knock-down kiosk for use at exhibitions and in other temporary locations. It is not known how many were made and, if any still remain, they are extremely well hidden.

Scott's concrete K3 was a success but, as the rate of installation increased, problems arose. The kiosks were produced by a number of manufacturers around Brit-ain and it was difficult to ensure the required standards. A Mark 2 version was introduced in 1934, featuring new moulding details and much thicker roof pillars, but it had become clear that, even though cast-iron boxes cost more to manufacture, the long-term maintenance costs were lower. In addition, not only were the K1 and K3 smaller externally than the K2 but, as their walls were thicker, their internal space was smaller still. What was

The style of lettering around the dome of the K2 was soon changed to this more elegant form. The same serif lettering, in maroon on cream, was used thereafter until the 1960s.

9

Left: *Two of the few K2s that were erected outside London. These were to be found in Oxford.*

Right: *The concrete K3 was used throughout the United Kingdom, on both urban and rural sites. An all-red colour scheme was allowed, but the most normal livery was cream stipple paint and red glazing bars. This box was outside the Belfast Post Office.*

Left: *Some places that demanded, but were denied, the K2 were very reluctant to accept the K1. A compromise was reached in Eastbourne with the provision of two specially thatched units.*

Right: *The modified K1 (the Mk236) provided the Post Office with a generally acceptable yet low-cost option. It shared the new standard 'Telephone' sign with the K2.*

The Kiosk No. 4 '24-hour post office'. Because it was about half as large again as the K2 and needed clear access to both ends, suitable sites were difficult to find. It was very expensive too. Only a single batch of fifty was ordered. (Left to right) Front elevation, side elevation, back elevation.

needed was a model with the small ground area of the K3 and the spacious interior of the K2.

Post Office engineers considered constructing the K3 in fabricated steel, making the walls much thinner. However, even as they were making their plans, a more pressing consideration arose. In 1935 King George V was to celebrate his Jubilee so, to mark the event, the Post Office commissioned a new 'Jubilee Kiosk' from Sir Giles Gilbert Scott. It would be in cast iron, it would be red, and it was to be for use everywhere. Designated the K6, it arrived on the streets in 1936.

Hitherto, whatever the design of kiosk, many communities had found it very difficult to persuade the Post Office to let them have one at all. In very many cases, particularly in rural areas, the Post Office would install a kiosk only if the local council agreed to cover all the Post Office's losses in providing and operat-

A sort of 'flat pack' kiosk, in metal-faced plywood, the K5 was intended for temporary use at exhibitions and events. This artist's impression was produced in 1987 using rediscovered working drawings.

The classic K6 'Jubilee Kiosk'. Introduced in 1936, it was to be Britain's standard kiosk for over thirty years. In that time around 60,000 were erected.

ing it. But now, along with the announcement of the Jubilee Kiosk, came a 'Jubilee Concession', by which henceforth call offices would be provided in every town and village with a post office, regardless of financial considerations. This concession led to over 8000 new kiosks being supplied.

In the following year, which marked the three hundredth anniversary of the Post Office, there was the 'Tercentenary Concession'. Under this scheme, if a local authority would pay £4 a year (then the normal residential subscription) for five years, the Post Office would provide a call office almost anywhere it was asked to. This scheme continued until 1949, and under it nearly 1000 more kiosks were erected.

The new K6 was also used to replace thousands of the older K1s and K3s. By the end of the 1930s, 20,000 K6s had been erected. The all-red kiosk became a familiar sight throughout Britain.

However, the K6 proved to be much to the liking of the criminal fraternity. Kiosk theft and vandalism had always been a problem (and still are), but many of the new boxes were in quiet locations, which made them especially vulnerable. The glazing frames could easily be removed with just an ordinary screwdriver, so that it was simple to collect enough glass to glaze a cold frame. Someone using a carefully positioned crowbar could easily wrench the cash box from the attractive but none too strong black and chrome backboard. To combat these

attacks, in 1939 a Mark 2 design was introduced. Its glazing frames were riveted in place and additional fixtures for the coinbox were included in the back panel of the kiosk. In order to take the cash box from a K6, a thief would have to destroy the kiosk.

Not everyone liked the red that had first become established as the standard colour for cast-iron boxes with the K2. Today the traditional red box is regarded as part of the British scene, but then it was not so. A bright red telephone box stood out rather too well for some people, especially those kiosks being put up in rural areas, where previously, if a community already had one, it was most probably cream. When a new kiosk was to be installed on an entirely new site, its bright red colour was going to stand out. The Post Office avoided making all but a very small number of exceptions to red but requests for other colours continued. In 1939 the Royal Fine Arts Commission was asked to look again at the question of colour. It endorsed the policy of red everywhere.

The Second World War halted mass production of K6s, although it proved possible to produce and install a further 2000 once the shortage of raw materials had eased. After the war a faster rate of installation resumed, although until 1950 it was still less than half of what it had been before the war.

In 1946, as the K6 again began to appear in significant numbers, and as town and country planning legislation began to proliferate, the Council for the Preservation of Rural England asked the Royal Fine Arts Commission to reconsider the insistence on the universal use of red.

The Post Office used the new Kiosk No. 6 to replace most of the concrete K3s. The reasons of lower maintenance costs and better provision for users were to be used again fifty years later when it was the K6's turn to be displaced.

S. SEED

"I got 'em cheap from the G.P.O."

The most convenient way to distinguish between a Mk1 and a Mk2 Kiosk No. 6 is to look at the back. If it has symmetrical cable entries, like this example, it is a pre-1939 Mk1. If the holes are asymmetrical (moved to the right), it is a Mk2. The identity of the manufacturer can also usually be found there. There are five: the Carron Foundry; Lion Foundry; Macfarlane (also known as Saracen Foundry); McDowall Steven; and Bratt Colbran.

This time the Commission relented. In areas of special beauty, dark grey or black could be used so long as the glazing bars were picked out in red. The dispute was not over yet, however. Questions were asked in Parliament and, within a year, the Postmaster General agreed to look at the issue yet again. Six kiosks were painted in different colours and placed on view for inspection. One was painted red, the others Deep Brunswick Green, Light Brunswick Green, black, Light Battleship Grey and Dark Battleship Grey. The five boxes which were not red had the glazing bars of their doors and of one other side picked out in red so that they could be viewed with or without the feature. The conclusion was that red should remain the standard colour for normal rural and urban sites, but that Dark Battleship Grey with red glazing bars could be used in places of exceptional natural beauty.

Colour was not the only source of complaint. The K6, like the K2 before it, carried the royal crown motif from the Post Office crest. With the death in 1952 of King George VI and the ascent to the throne of Queen Elizabeth II, the Post Office changed this motif to represent the St Edward's Crown adopted by the new

13

Although the model was pre-war, most K6s were installed after the war. The peak rate was in the late 1940s and early 1950s, when kiosks represented one of the few means the government had of extending the telephone service.

The St Edward's Crown was first introduced on K6s in 1953. The 'slot' detail introduced in 1955 to placate the Scots provides a convenient means of identifying post-1955 kiosks. Integral St Edward's Crowns date a K6 to between 1953 and 1955.

The Queen's Crown of Scotland, as fitted after 1955 into K6s destined for use north of the border. At least one of these crowns is known to have travelled south. A K6 outside Wembley Stadium sported a mixture of crowns.

monarch. It was soon pointed out that, contrary to what the new crown implied (and letter boxes announced in the cipher E II R), Her Majesty was not the second Queen Elizabeth of Scotland and that the new Post Office crest did not apply north of the border. The solution was introduced in 1955. Henceforth, K6 fascias were to be cast with slots, into which either the Queen's Crown of Scotland or the St Edward's Crown would be inserted before the roof was fitted, depending on where the box was destined to be used.

Between 1950 and 1955 about 25,000 new K6s were erected, an even greater rate than before 1939. The pace slowed thereafter, but they were still being installed at the rate of about a thousand a year in the mid 1960s.

The GPO again considered the possibility of a new design of kiosk and in 1958 invited designs from three noted designers and architects, Neville Conder, Misha Black and Jack Howe. All three proposed to use aluminium. The GPO

Neither red, nor grey, nor carrying a crown motif, the white kiosks in Hull have always had their own unique style.

A post-1955 K6 in the alternative grey and red livery, in the Cathedral Close at Salisbury.

eventually selected Conder's design for a field trial. It was designated the K7, and the first versions were erected in 1962. The K7 was innovative in many ways. It was determinedly modern and was intended to be erected in groups, by then an increasingly likely need. It used windows fixed in rubber gaskets, much like those used for many years for car windscreens. Six prototypes were made, five of which entered public service. These were in aluminium, as Conder had intended, but they lacked some of the machined surface finishes that would be possible with mass-production. Most of these were designed to combat the effect of weathering on aluminium and, in their absence, the Post Office was soon criticising the material as unsuitable for the British climate. It is also very possible that Post Office engineers were reluctant to adopt a new ma-

15

By the end of the 1950s, as demand grew, kiosks were frequently grouped, often by the addition of boxes to an existing site. This elegant group in Stafford is of three pre-1953 units and one that is post-1955.

terial. Without telling Conder what they were doing, they commissioned a further half dozen K7s in cast iron. What happened to this second batch is not known. It is reported that some were erected in Glasgow, but this remains unconfirmed. Whatever happened to them, the K7 was not adopted for general use and most of the aluminium prototypes went on to provide perfectly satisfactory service for twenty years.

The Post Office preference for cast iron continued in the design that eventually superseded the K6. It was not that the K6 needed to be replaced, but there was a need for a more modern design that was suitable for use in the many new town centres and housing estates being built, and that was cheaper to produce, easier to maintain and resistant to the greatly increased levels of vandalism.

Five aluminium K7s were put on trial in 1962. One was in Coventry, another in the City of London. These three were in Grosvenor Gardens, near Victoria station, London.

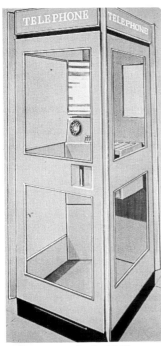

Left: *The main material for Douglas Scott's submission was cast iron. Stainless steel was used for the corner cappings and for the glazing frames.*

Right: *One of the very first K8s, photographed on the day of its public launch in 1968. Notice the new plain lettering and the lack of any crown motif.*

Consequently, in 1965, a new competition was held for what was to become the K8. Three designers were asked to submit proposals – Neville Conder, Bruce Martin and Douglas Scott. In the end, only Martin and Scott produced complete designs. Martin's was to be made in aluminium. Scott's was to use cast iron. Martin's design was preferred, but the Post Office was concerned that it might not be strong enough, so they made it of cast iron but with a cast aluminium door. It first appeared on the streets in July 1968.

The K8 was a fundamentally different design to the K6 and it also incorporated a more subtle change: it was not quite the same shade of red. The K8 was 'poppy red' (BS381C – red 539, to be precise), a slightly more orange shade than the old Post Office red (BS381C – red 538). Over the following years the new livery was applied to all kiosks.

This group of K8s sports the early 1980s experimental and controversial yellow livery of the newly established British Telecom.

MODERN TIMES

The 1970s were a period of relative stability. Compared with the previous forty years, the number of new kiosks installed was small. Some new sites were opened, for which the K8 was used, and when kiosks needed moving or where vandalism became a serious problem the existing unit would usually be replaced with the current model. Around 4000 K8s were supplied.

The K8 was more resistant to attack than its predecessor, but the degree of improvement was not enough to justify replacement of all the threatened K6s. In many instances the Post Office took a dramatic approach and ripped out the original glazing frames before the vandals did, replacing them with K8-style single-pane windows, the portion up to knee height being filled with sheet steel. The toughened glass that had been used for many years was replaced by unbreakable polycarbonate. Unhappily this scratched easily and became opaque through damage and frequent efforts to remove graffiti. The modified boxes looked ugly but it had become extremely difficult to keep the payphones working. In the circumstances, the appearance of the kiosks was of little importance to those needing to make an emergency call.

Another solution was to use a more open, 'walk-up' booth. The first of these was the 'Booth 7A', called the Oakham, after the Old Oak ham tin, which it resembled. The idea originated at a meeting on Tyneside, where staff from Post Office headquarters in London were told stories of kiosks that had been set ablaze and of others being dragged away by lines attached to lorries, the thieves preferring to break open the cash box somewhere less public. One of the local team ob-

The Booth 7A was known as the 'Oakham', because it resembled an Old Oak ham tin. It had no lighting of its own and was painted bright yellow to make it more visible.

served that what was needed was something made like a battleship, perhaps built by the local Swan Hunter shipyard. The headquarters team continued the discussions on the train home, and by the time they arrived back in London they had completed the basic design of the Oakham.

The first unit was erected in 1980, in Gateshead, and it was soon appearing elsewhere. It proved to be a highly successful design and even survived intact the inner city riots of the early 1980s. The Oakham was painted yellow, partly because it had no lighting of its own and red was not felt to be sufficiently visible. The brighter colour was, however, about to take on a new significance.

When Post Office Telecommunications and the Royal Mail were separated in readiness for privatisation, new corporate identities were established. British Telecom, the trading identity of the new telecommunications company, adopted a blue and yellow colour scheme. As an experiment, some telephone boxes were painted yellow. It was not a popular move! It soon became clear that the British held the red telephone box on a par with black taxi cabs. Yellow was simply not acceptable. In the end, and at least in part because the new colour showed the dirt more easily, British Telecom decided to limit the use of yellow to the K8, and then only if local people wished to make the change. Few did.

Meanwhile, other more fundamental discussions had been under way. The cast-iron boxes could be expected to last for another forty years or more but the way

18

A very sad K8, photographed in 1985 in East London. The steel props were not there to hold the roof up, but to stop users falling through the missing windows should they lean on them. The payphone was still working when the picture was taken.

in the 1979 report. His designs reached prototype stage only. They had been produced to suit production at the rate of 10,000 a year. In the lead up to British Telecom's privatisation financial constraints had reduced the forecast demand to less than a tenth of this, and the DCA designs would no longer be economic. Attention turned to an internally designed range known as the 'Croydon'. Based loosely on the DCA designs, this, too, went to prototype stage and no further. There was another change of plan.

payphones were used was changing. Accessibility for disabled users was becoming an important consideration, for example. It was time to have a thorough review of the telephone box. In 1979 a study reported that all the various needs could be satisfied by a range of six models: a conventional kiosk with a door, a similar unit without a door, a walk-up booth in both floor- and wall-mounted forms, a robust Oakham-style pedestal structure, and a variant of one or other of these designed to suit the disabled.

Over the next couple of years, a number of new models were tried out. Some were imported from Europe and North America. Some were new British designs. They were of several shapes, some open, others closed, and none were of cast iron. Meanwhile British Telecom commissioned David Carter of DCA Design Consultants to develop a range of housings as defined

The King 511, from Canada, installed near Holborn Circus, London. Described in the literature as providing 'fresh solutions', it was constructed of aluminium and acrylic.

19

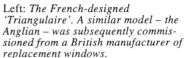

Left: *The French-designed 'Triangulaire'. A similar model – the Anglian – was subsequently commissioned from a British manufacturer of replacement windows.*

Below: *The KX100, in British Telecom livery. These have frequently been installed in pairs.*

Above: *Prototypes of the 'Croydon' range lined up for inspection in July 1985.*

The payphone service was in trouble. The widespread unreliability of call boxes through vandalism and failure to repair damage speedily was a major public concern and an acute embarrassment to the newly privatised British Telecom. In 1985 it announced a major programme to rectify the situation. Payphones were to be transformed, and one aspect of this was to be the widespread use of a new 'KX' range of housings.

British Telecom was enthusiastic about its new designs, describing them as attractive, functional and modern. For the company, the use of stainless steel and anodised aluminium meant the end of routine painting. Regular cleaning would be all that was needed to maintain their appearance. They were also expected to be more resistant to vandalism and theft and so easier to keep in operation. There were

A publicity shot of the KX420. The style of the photograph fails to convey its main purpose, namely to supersede the Oakham on sites in vulnerable locations.

practical improvements for the user, too. None of the new models had a step to climb when entering, the doors were much easier to open, and the lighting was much brighter than in any predecessor.

Those who used the new designs were generally satisfied with what they offered. There might be a draught around one's ankles, but at least one did not have to step through rubbish to use the telephone and it stayed clean and in working order for rather longer. Nevertheless, the welcome was not universal. Some dismissed the new designs as little more than glazed boxes. Many were more concerned about the wholesale replacement of the older 'traditional' red boxes.

In July 1988 a new telecommunications company, Mercury Communications, then the only other licensed network operator, opened a rival public payphone service.

A nest of triangular KX300s at Newport Pagnell motorway services on the M1. This versatile unit could be used in many arrangements and was available with the payphone either on the pillar or on a panelled side.

Far left: *The Mercury booth, by Machin. Like most designs before it, the initial detailing was changed as the result of experience. 'Telephone' signs were added to the roof and most have been fitted with low-level guard rails.*

Left: *A double KX200 in 1990s BT livery. It was often possible to use the double unit to replace a single old-style kiosk.*

Left: *A typical pair of 1990s KX100s in Tottenham Court Road, London, where there are dozens of telephone boxes. The availability of credit-card telephones necessitated the introduction of several other signs.*

Right: *This experimental unit, also in Tottenham Court Road, was erected by Mercury in early 1994.*

New telephone companies bring with them new identities. These boxes, at Newport Pagnell motorway services, were erected by Paytelco. Cable television companies have also joined the fray, with the first being opened by Euro Bell, in Crawley, in late 1993.

Three housing designs were launched with the heavily publicised opening of 26 sites on Waterloo station, London. One was an open booth, designed by Machin, intended mainly for open sites. The second design, by Fitch & Company, was for a range of indoor models suited to shopping malls, railway stations and similar situations. Both were intended for use either in groups or singly, and subsequently both were widely used. The third design, a classically styled concept by John Simpson, was for a range of kiosk-style housings, but this was not adopted.

Meanwhile, the KX installation programme continued at full speed, although by this time it was mainly concentrated on providing kiosks at new sites rather than changing older housings. The original smoked glass, which had made the boxes almost invisible in some locations, was replaced by clear glass, with more prominent signs. Britain's public telephone service – and its telephone boxes – had been transformed in little more than five years.

British Telecom became BT in the early 1990s and, with this, the livery of the KXs changed when the British Telecom 'T' logos were replaced by the BT piper. Some sites are now occupied by a fourth generation of Post Office or BT box, and this is unlikely to be the last. Many more Mercury boxes are appearing, increasingly away from city-centre sites, and new housings continue to be tried out. New operators are establishing their presence on the street, and the growth in use of mobile telephones might one day mean that there is no need for payphones at all.

Only one thing is sure: the story of the telephone box is not over yet.

A much photographed set of preserved K2s, off Bow Street in London WC2. The group developed over time: the two on the right are dated 1926; the centre unit is 1930; the remaining two are 1931 and 1934 respectively.

PRESERVED KIOSKS

As the older K series boxes were replaced by the new KX models, there was a surge of nostalgia for what was about to disappear. To some extent the arguments for the retention of the red box had been rehearsed when British Telecom experimented with the use of yellow, but this time it was a matter of the boxes themselves disappearing forever. There would be no going back and the two sides in the battle that ensued – for that is what it became – were as polarised as they could have been. The preservationists would grasp any opportunity to support their cause and British Telecom, for its part, was not beyond turning out at dead of night to remove an old box and replace it with a new one.

The stand-off did not last long, and agreement was soon reached that about 2000 red boxes would be declared 'listed buildings'; in this special case the rules were altered to allow for structures as young as thirty years to be listed. At the time about one in twenty K6s were not old enough to be listed but, as age was difficult to determine, this fine detail was generally ignored. However, no K8s could be listed. Of the remaining red boxes, many have been left as they were: the economics of replacing an old housing simply for the sake of it are much as they have always been, so, for the foreseeable future, rather more than just the 2000 'listed' boxes will remain in service.

The rest – and by far the most – were sold off, mostly as largely complete units, but in some cases for scrap. Public auctions were held and recycled boxes began to appear in yards and gardens throughout Britain. Many were bought by dealers, some of whom amassed fields full of boxes to be restored and sold all over the world. Often the idea has been to restore the boxes to their original glory, with period interiors. Others have been converted to uses as varied as gatekeepers' lodges, cocktail bars, book shelves and fish tanks. Some have found use in nightclubs and restaurants as housings for payphones!

Meanwhile, many of the preserved boxes were spruced up and, in the process, some were changed from grey to red. Where grey was once the only acceptable colour in places of special beauty, red is now the required colour. It is odd, too, that many K6s now sport gold-painted crowns, a feature that is entirely new, yet in many areas BT has not been allowed to put 'Phonecard' signs in them, on the

A fine example of preservation in situ. This 1931 vintage K2 can be seen in Austin Friars, London EC2.

Most kiosk groups developed as the years passed and bulk installations were not routine until the 1960s. This group, adjacent to the old Stratford Town Hall, in East London, probably dates from around 1950 and is unusual in that all three appear to have been installed together.

This atmospheric photograph of the early 1990s is deceptive. The KX housing (near) was erected before the K2 (rear). Marking the first – and largely unnoticed – appearance of red boxes in Parliament Square, the K2 has since been joined by several refurbished K6s, one of which replaced the KX in this picture.

Two incorrect details to look out for: many K6s carry signs with the wrong style of lettering, a consequence of lax transcription when production drawings were reissued, and many K6s now have their crowns picked out, usually in gold. What would Giles Gilbert Scott have thought? (The lettering, at least, is corrected when new signs have to be installed.)

grounds that this is not an original detail.

Perhaps the strangest twist of all has been the re-installation of red boxes in some sites. The most notable example of this has been in the City of Westminster, which, in late 1993 gained an extra sixty or so recycled K6s to add to its existing one hundred listed boxes. About half of the new 'old' boxes replaced KX units. The remainder were on fresh sites in prominent or cramped locations where previously the idea of a telephone box had been unthinkable, such as in White-hall and Trafalgar Square, outside the Waldorf Hotel and on the narrow pavements of the eastern end of the Strand.

Not all kiosks have been used for public telephones. Some have been bought for use as telephone cabinets on factory sites. Others have been used on railway stations as announcer's booths. This K8 owned by London Underground (in pale yellow) is on Whitechapel station.

27

Not all public telephones are in street kiosks. Many are in booths in railway stations, airports and other public places. This elegant 1930s suite was at Charing Cross station, London.

YOU MAY TELEPHONE FROM HERE

The telephone companies were not the only bodies to provide telephone boxes: the emergency services and motoring organisations have also done so.

The Automobile Association (AA) and Royal Automobile Club (RAC) began their networks of boxes in 1912-13, when their strategically positioned patrolmen were provided with wooden sentry boxes to protect them from the weather. The AA quickly began installing telephones to provide a link back to headquarters and also to allow for members' messages to be passed on. The RAC followed suit in 1919 and soon both organisations were erecting boxes along main routes, principally for the benefit of passing members. There was no coinbox, as such. Local calls were free. An honesty box was provided for trunk-call fees.

The first boxes were simple wooden structures, although later models were rather more ornate. The AA's 'Super Telephone Boxes' installed in the late 1920s were 6 feet (1.8 metres) square and almost 13 feet (4.0 metres) high, with a further 10 foot (3.0 metre) long illuminated signpost pole on top! By the mid 1940s the two networks totalled over a thousand sites and, from 1947, members were able to use both systems. The move to pedestal-style call points began in the early 1960s, with trials of directly linked emergency telephones, such as had been installed on the new M1 motorway. Standard pedestal units, using fibreglass and steel, were introduced in 1968 and these and their successors now form the bulk of the networks. Forty or so of the older boxes still remain, mostly dating from the 1950s and almost all of them AA boxes.

Motorway emergency call points have never been anything other than pedestal booths. The first were housed in extremely primitive rectangular boxes designed by the Ministry of Transport. The unit in use in 1994, although still more functional than attractive, is a vast improvement.

Police call points allowed officers on patrol to keep in touch with the local police station in the days before personal radios. A light on the top would flash to attract the attention of a passing policeman. The public were invited to use the telephones, both in emergencies and for more routine queries. Styles varied, with some being specific to an individual force, although a degree of standardisation came about in the 1930s. The housings took two main forms. Most were simple cast-iron pillars containing a telephone and a separate lockable cupboard in which useful items like first-aid material could be kept. The other main style was a large kiosk, made of concrete, which gained fame in the *Doctor Who* television series as the 'Tardis'. The space inside was big enough to provide a convenient lock-up for villains awaiting transfer to the cells.

Several police call points have been preserved, most of them in museums or at police training centres. Glasgow still retains several of the 'Tardis' type and Edinburgh has some of its own local version. The City of London retains some of its light blue pillars, and there are two in Metropolitan Police dark blue in the City of Westminster. One of these is in Piccadilly Circus, and it is not all that it seems. It is a former City Police box, disguised as a 'Met' one, the original listed box having been dug out of the ground and stolen at some time during the late 1980s.

Below left: *Although AA boxes looked much the same as each other, it was not until 1956 that the AA standardised the design.*

Below right: *A somewhat functional RAC box at Ellerbeck on the edge of the North York Moors, photographed in the mid 1980s.*

The City of London has preserved several of its old light blue police pillars. This unusual unit, under restoration when photographed, is in Old Broad Street, EC2.

Above: *A 'Tardis' police box, pictured at South Mimms, Hertfordshire, in 1979. Boxes of this type were first erected in London in 1930. They were installed in the outer London districts; posts were used in inner London. The box was designed so that a person could stand inside. By 1953, there were 685 of these boxes, but with the introduction of personal police radios they were phased out from 1969 onwards.*

Not all large police boxes looked like the 'Tardis'. This one can be seen in Almondbury, near Huddersfield.

FURTHER READING

Aslet, C., and Powers, A. *The British Telephone Box – Take It As Red.* The Thirties Society, London, 1987.
Bunker, John. *From Rattle to Radio.* Brewin Books, 1988.
'CWM'. 'Bloomsbury and Its Kiosks', *Telegraph and Telephone Journal* (October 1927), 10-11.
Gray, John. 'GPO Miscellany', *Design*, February 1959.
Judd, F. J. 'Kiosks', *Post Office Electrical Engineers' Journal,* volume 29 (October 1936), 175-7.
Martin, B. 'The Smallest Building – The Genesis of the Mark 8 Telephone Box', *RIBA Journal*, volume 76 (August 1969), 320-5.
Moore, M. B.; Maile, J. L.; and Martin, B. 'A New Telephone Kiosk – Kiosk No. 8', *Post Office Electrical Engineers' Journal*, volume 62 (April 1969), 54-6.
Orchin, George. 'You May Telephone From Here', *Post Office Telecommunications Journal* (1954), 105-10.
Robinson, O. 'Call Offices Worked by Attendants', *The National Telephone Journal* (March 1911), 248-9.
Stamp, Gavin. *Telephone Boxes.* Chatto & Windus, 1989.
Timpson, John. *Requiem for a Red Box.* Pyramid, 1989.

In addition, the BT Museum (telephone 071-248 7447), BT Archives (telephone 071-822 1002) and the British Architectural Library of the Royal Institute of British Architects (telephone 071-580 5533) hold collections of related material. Information on specific sites can often be found in local council minutes. Local and national newspapers provide a further valuable source.

PLACES TO VISIT

It is impossible to list all the places that might be visited. Every site has its own story and even the most selective list of highlights would fill several books. Here are the major museums and four personal favourites. Opening times, admission charges and visitor facilities vary, so please check before making a journey.

Avoncroft Museum of Buildings, Redditch Road, Stoke Heath, Bromsgrove, Worcestershire B60 4JR. Telephone: 0527 831886. The National Telephone Kiosk Collection, with examples of almost all K series boxes including a reconstruction of a K5. A selection of modern boxes completes by far the best display in the United Kingdom.
Bradford Industrial Museum, Moorside Road, Eccleshill, Bradford, West Yorkshire BD2 3HP. Telephone: 0274 631756. Has a K2 and the only known surviving pre-K series box, a 'Wilson A'.
BT Museum, 145 Queen Victoria Street, London EC4V 4AT. Telephone: 071-248 7444. Displays include a fully fitted 1950s K6 and a City of London Police pillar. Research library (telephone 071-248 7447) available by appointment.
National Motor Museum, John Montagu Building, Beaulieu, Brockenhurst, Hampshire SO42 7ZN. Telephone: 0590 612345. AA and RAC boxes.
National Tramway Museum, Crich, Matlock, Derbyshire DE4 5DP. Telephone: 0773 852565. A growing collection includes a K1 Mk235, a police pillar and a 'Tardis'.
Oxford Telecom Museum, 35 Speedwell Street, Oxford OX1 1RH. Telephone: 0865 246601. Strictly by appointment only, a small display includes a K1 Mk236 and a K7.
Science Museum, Exhibition Road, South Kensington, London SW7 2DD. Telephone: 071-938 8000. The telecommunications gallery includes a K3.

Other public locations of particular interest include:

Kingston-upon-Thames, Surrey. A sculpture in the town centre is formed out of a dozen K6s.

Liverpool Anglican Cathedral. A K6 by Sir Giles Gilbert Scott inside his great cathedral.

Rhynd, near Perth, Scotland. The only remaining K3 Mk2.

Royal Academy of Arts, Burlington House, Piccadilly, London W1V 0DS. Telephone: 071-439 7438. A pair of working boxes, one a regular K2, the other the wooden prototype of Scott's design.

A splendid example of kiosk preservation. This K4 can be seen at Cranmore station, on the East Somerset Railway.